One Daughter Is Worth Ten Sons

One Daughter Is
Worth Ten Sons

Jiwon Choi

Hanging Loose Press
Brooklyn, New York

Published by Hanging Loose Press, 231 Wyckoff Street, Brooklyn, New York 11217-2208. All rights reserved. No part of this book may be reproduced without the publisher's written permission, except for brief quotations in reviews.

www.hangingloosepress.com

Printed in the United States of America
10 9 8 7 6 5 4 3 2 1

Hanging Loose Press thanks the Literature Program of the New York State Council on the Arts for a grant in support of the publication of this book.

Cover art: Portrait of the poet, her 100-day photo. The Korean custom of celebrating the 100th day of a baby's life stems from the pre-modern era when medical care was scarce and crude, and the infant mortality rate was high. Parents would keep their infants indoors and refrain from receiving visitors until their child made it to the magic number of 100 days.

Cover design: Marie Carter

Acknowledgments
Bombay Gin Journal: "Koreans in Proverbs: Literal Meanings
        in a Series"
Hanging Loose: "All Roads Lead to Rockaway Beach 143rd"; "1977:
        Kiddieland, the Devil and My Dorothy Hamill Bangs"; "Cortes
        Takes the 'R' Train"
Painted Bride Quarterly (online): "I Pay My Book Fine"; "Jane Austen,
        reconsider"
Rosebud Magazine: "Korean Grocery" (co-winner of the William
        Stafford Prize)

ISBN 978-1-934909-98-0

Library of Congress cataloging-in-publication data available on request.

For My Father

Contents

Koreans in Proverbs: Expect a Petulant God

A beautiful wild apricot
빛 좋은 개살구

Looking for love
is what keeps you
picking losers

how many times
will you spit
out the pit and never
eat the fruit?

Shake anyone and dust will fall off
털어서 먼지 안 나는 사람 없다

Cinderella
in the dumps
on your knees
with your heart stapled
to your half-sleeve

your fat sisters
spend the whole day
dipping fat fingers into
the peanut butter crock

anaphylaxis is too good
for them, but a dead rat
under their pillow
might be just the thing.

A mouse trapped in a jar
독 안에 든 쥐

Hope:
she's not for the faint-hearted
expect
a petulant god
meting out justice
she has no time for kindness
no use for your allegiance

and please not another sob story
about your dog, pony or wife . . .

it's time you learned to grin
and bear it.

ONE

HOW WILL I KNOW I WAS ALIVE?

All Roads Lead to Rockaway Beach 143rd

i.

Archangel of Neponsit

The B-list god wears his crown
hard-won and aluminum
to let me know his lineage
of whisky-in-the-jar-o
compels him to pick an Irish Rose
one of those girls who ruled
his schnapps-fueled nights
of nineteen eighty-four
dancing topless around bonfires
and mistaking planes
for stars

I wish on these
same impostor stars
one by one
willing the night sky
to swallow me
whole.

ii.

She

She grew up
tall and translucent
singing along
with the North Sea

chanteys of men
carved from stone
and women a'wings
wondering if she
should check for a knot
where scapulars
used to be.

Black Irish
glow in the dark
she leaves off the light
when she puts her face
to the mirror to pick
at the spot on her chin
that has nothing to do
with beauty.

She was five
when she got
it wasn't coming off
no matter how hard
she rubbed or plucked.
Was it a mark left
by the Devil's quill
or an angel's pen?

It is the randomness
that keeps her up
at night.

iii.

In Korean Years

Five of mine to one of yours
is what it will take
to get over you
to get your ocean out of my nose
and ears and get my eyes
to blacken your skies blue

you were my pirate on land
in your Gaelic house
tart with wenches
sloppy with first mates
we walked the plank to splinters
my bonny boy of the northeast
swampland

you are the last stone
I can't shake out of my shoe
but you let me leave
with a limp
not entirely free
do you ever think of me?
Send me a signal—
a drunken gull, a lonely pigeon
with a note tied around
her flank or the least you can do
is shove a piece of paper
into an empty bottle.

Of The Wild

It's ridiculous now but she recalls
the afternoon when she was sixteen
tugging at turnips, salt-sweat
stinging her eyes, out of breath
when she heard the doorbell.
The wolf had been waiting.

She had not seen him coming,
the most odious one covered in blood,
the wolf she married. And all these years of ever after,
she's still here darning socks, gutting fish,
tending their misshapen cruel children

who she unlatches and watches
as they run to the far dunes to plunder
plover eggs. The wolf will not get up
until high noon and by then she will have pushed away
land and sea to be closer to heaven
than anyone can imagine.

In the end her struggle is not with drowning,
but her own infamy: who will remember she wrestled
trees for their fruit and growled back at the black forest?
Will you remember that her hair was more copper
than copper and her breath sweeter
than wild honeysuckle?

How Will I Know I Was Alive?

for Philip Levine

i.

Lay me
sloth
under a pile of leaves
free from the desire
to deconstruct Rumi
or the perfect banana cream pie
until genetic forces and the Big Bang
conspire to make me
what I am

morbid
dreaming in blood
of broken bodies
and my ghosts fully formed.

ii.

My flesh
your flesh
our nature is
animal.

What is human?

Sad rhetoric and theories
leading to assassinations
in Texas

napalm in Cambodia
look what they did to Lumumba
in Congo.

God made me
with a hole in my heart
but you say
it was evolution.

iii.

They dig up bones
all the time
under shopping malls
and car parks

mandible
femur
ulna

pieces of the puzzle
when butterflies
slumbered in amber
and men were made of mountains.

The story about the time traveler
who falls up a hole in the street
is true. He falls in love with a librarian who finds him
staring at neon signs.
She takes him home for
a tuna sandwich.

iv.

When I was eight I walked the bottom
of some guy's pool at a party on Long Island
looking for that trick door into Atlantis
where I would live out my mermaid's tale
in a fortress of kelp and coral
trapping wide-eyed sailors for my kettle
burying conquistadors
and digging up Blackbeard's gold

(the topless thing might be awkward, but so is watching
        the Lawrence Welk Show
every Saturday night with my father).

v.

I don't want to be a memory

floating up into the sky.

What was it all for?

On the Island of Gleaming Blackness

The Sirens rule your tendons
and lower regions with eyes painted in
by Poseidon
and lips like the Northern Lights:
quick to catch fire

in your castle bedlam
you conjure these heavy-breasted
half-beast women in dreams
and etch them on your walls
like a caveman scribing in
mastodons and saber-tooths.

You poor
stay-at-home college grad
bastard whose mummy
still washes his drawers.
You've become one of those
fish-eaten dead walking,
spit back into to your milquetoast life.
Not a zombie.
Just a broken boy.

Rat

i.

he appears
a shrunken pony
easing passage
across asphalt plains
and concrete tundras
into the green flash
of the setting sun

ii.

our dead lie
in their eternal hour
sod coming out
of every orifice—what do plastic flowers
matter to a child who died
not yet weaned
from his mother's teat?

rat's underground empire
is bones
gnawed free from old men and new babies—
the pharaohs had their stone
but rat has our bones

iii.

rat finds her
inside a rib cage

rustling in
parcels
of quarter cobs
half bagels
and tomatoes

he is smitten

consummation
should be easy
as eating a chicken wing
and sipping on beer
but *not so fast, buddy*
she makes him promise
not to let the jib
get away from the boat

iv.

tossed
over a garden
fence, your tail
twitching alive
with black ants

Time Works

I am a harpy
so sharply
whetted

a blade
rubbed against
an ice age

of moraine
honed into
a lizard disposition

under
a mammalian
extension

my monster
insides
are a wonder

of guts—
neon spleens
and gizzards

knowing time
works
if you let it

disappear
suns and planes
into cloud dimensions

returning us
to our prehistoric
age.

Cortes Takes the "R" Train

The Sun made us
by pulling out her smallest teeth
and spitting these
onto Earth
where we became rocks
and trees
some of us sinking
to the bottom of the sea
where we fulfilled our Atlantis destiny
growing gills
and mermaid's scales

it was the beginning
and we had no thoughts
just the ambition of cells
to split and split again
growing our matter
into mass: mothers into
daughters

it makes no difference
that it was you
Cortes
they sent to collect our gold
a worker bee doing the queen's bidding
growing the legless, blind worms
into a galleon of cannons
and fire

when you landed
you showed us how little you knew
about genus:

Neanderthals
Ancient Sumerians
Aztec Indians

all of us
thrust into the fire
like wild pigs
until our eyes melted
and our hearts exploded
like Roman candles
in the night

but we crossed the centuries to be here
to grow like corn
to show the Mayan ruins
in our ancient faces
riding through Queens
on the "R" train.

Memoir Mori

In Part One, I will introduce my mother, butcher-in-chief
feasting on her young, bones and gristle, sauté
and sizzle with toothsome glee. Day-old tabloid soup
moving you on to

Part Two where I make my escape to a liberal arts college
and become afflicted with a condition known as *poetry-writing*
where I Ouija-board Plath nightly for instruction on restitution
and virgin suicides.

In Part Three I seek solace in philosophy (I fuck
therefore I am) also known as impersonating Freudian slips:
you're not a family until you're a tragedy.
How to begin Part Four?

Cue the tall, blond Tourette's syndrome, a foolish moth
trapped inside my self-loathing. I pull his wings right off.
Must I make meaning of my stint at the 7-Eleven roasting wieners
for pimply boys seeking nirvana in Hot Pockets and Ding Dongs?

If I leave salvation unwritten, will it come in?

I Take the "D" Train

From Stillwell Avenue
to Rockefeller Center
the Fujianese
Guyanese
Uzbekistanis
hum and flow
tongues in flux
vowels in absentia

our human mass
in transit

then I spy the half-eaten
pastrami on rye
gutted and strewn
under the seat and I grieve
for this tale of unrequited lunch.

Let's Go Out Tonight

Charging from one neck of the woods to another
the cab driver pushes our chariot from one pothole to another
over patches of pigeons while the radio bleeds the blues

"Is that Blind Lemon?" I ask

"Lightnin' Hopkins," he says

"But Blind Lemon liked Hopkins to play with him sometimes," I add

"How come you know about that?" he turns to look at me

He is an older black man, forehead furrowed with Socrates's worries

"I like the blues," I reply

By the time we pull up to the curb John Lee Hooker is cajoling

"Let's go out tonight!"

so I pay my fare and do just that.

In Korean Years

If I stretched out my arm, I could pick
the ripe red persimmons.
                    —Byungu Chon, "Falling Persimmons"

i.

Persimmon

I ate your sorrow
expecting bitter
but there was none

no ocean of tears
collecting
since the beginning
with Adam then Eve
tossed out of Eden
like a sack of apples
from the cellar
gone on too long
lackluster
and not what God
intended.

Your sorrow fallen
from a tree
growing on a hard lean
gives the most forlorn
fruit.

I ate your sorrow
and it was persimmon.

ii.

Mackerel and Green Cabbage

The last day you'd see your mother's bright eyes and hear your father
say your name was the journey over mountains leading to the city
of your new orphanhood. You were twelve and your sister told you

to pack a bag, but leave everything except all the food you could carry.
You left your books and clothes, and your best red hen—
      the only one in
the clutch who didn't run when you came around with millet and
      apple skins.

When you became American you watched that movie thinking you
      were Dorothy.
But no, you were the house torn from its foundation and the years you
spent trying to fit in were the flying monkeys. And by the way,

only Americans would follow a brick road, throw water on a witch,
      and tap red slippers
three times to get back to the kitchen where mother is putting
mackerel and green cabbage on the table.

iii.

Crackers

After school
find me on the sofa
with Ritz on my lap
doing homework in proper
fourth grade fashion:

pencil no. 2 and bubblegum-scented eraser
dueling it out in my notebook
while Erik Estrada straddles
the California highway.

Back to 1951

My father is forgetting my face as he lies dying
in the company of parrots in bright eye shadow and lips
like Christmas.
On a battery of wings, surrounded by a halo of flies,
he is lifted back to 1951, seventeen and hiding in the mountains,
living off bitter roots and small snakes,
giving the Red Army the finger.

He stayed there long after soldiers went back to their farm
and factory lives
while I tried to fit inside his tin can of a heart:

thou shalt not smoke
thou shalt not skip breakfast
thou shalt not end up an old maid . . .

Did Confucius say headstrong daughters must assume
            the venerable position?

Do it anyway: kowtow and contemplate remains of flesh and bone
melting into silt and soil.

Curse

The old man
on the side of the road
is an armadillo
letting go
the slippery tail
of his life

he was a husk
of a man
who lived
as a tight-eyed
creature, burrowing in
darkness
embedded in
silence

he never claimed me
as kin
but my face says
I am of him

nose
sharp enough
to cut a loaf
eyebrows
à la caterpillar
and the inkblot
on my chin
that came on
like a curse

I am his
prickly rose
clinging to
shadows
because
that is all
I know.

The Poet

He is
a stray cat
a gutted eye-socket
leading to
dark spaces
inside.
I look at him
in this room
with just a light
bulb dangling
and hold my breath
it's Horror Movie 101—
expect a hatchet
any moment

but all that happens
is he brings in
the morbid
when he pulls out
the *Iliad*
and pulls on
his Four Roses
insisting
the Murderous Dream
rages
from the heavy pages
and Achilles
will not be
appeased!

The poet must
conjure reckonings
at all cost.

Koreans In Proverbs: *Carpe Diem*

Entrust the cat with the fish
고양이에게 생선을 맡기다

Oh King of the night
kitchen
maw well suited
for carpe diem
heads
severed from
fish-bodies
tossed into
the corner bucket
where your tribute
awaits you.

Test the bridge before crossing it
돌다리도 두드러 보고 건너라

The ghost at the foot
of your bed has black hair
just like your mother
when she used to be
smooth and plastic

could it be the afterlife
is good for your skin?

she has come from
this Dimension of the Dead
to transmit a message:

you must learn to fall.

TWO
NO REGRETS

I Pay My Book Fine

I have kept you
Ko Un
for days longer
than the iron-bound librarian
allows.

You are the poet
of magpies—they sleep
on your shoulders
just out of winter's cruel reach
undisturbed
by millet shortages
and so many tiny burials.

Travelers
on these old village roads
cherish their walk
through the world
and you write about them
with the ink of your veins.

Auspicious
was the Spring you met
the inn owner's daughter and took her
into the mountains
hoping to glimpse the moon
only to be confounded by the knot
of her sash.

Though I leave you
in the RETURNS cart
I won't stop
I will Ko Un.

Anne Sexton & Flying Monkeys

She is perfect mink hair
framing perfect horse teeth
come to unleash
the guilt-loving mothers
and boozy uncles who clutter
our ordinary childhoods

she expects we'll jump
on broomsticks
to rein in the anarchy
of sad memories
but we are no match
for these flying monkeys

she says she can see us
under the red lipstick
that bloodens our teeth

but we see her too:

a girl waiting in the rain
for a wolf
who will not show
while her socks
get wet.

The Hag

i.

our house:
stale gingerbread
glued together
with hard icing
starlings peck off
when they think we are
gone

but the hag is always here
aiming her slingshot at their sharp
beaks and numb skulls—
when she's got them in a pile
feathers and innards all go into
a pie

she is hungry all the time
cannot fill her black hole
ever deeper, ever wider
each year waiting to die

ii.

her bottomless pot
is a porridge of the swamp—
of toads, large rats,
unsuspecting huntsmen
stuffed into her kettle
and down into our gullets

we never used to have a taste
for flesh

iii.

we came here with our father
after our mother died
back when the hag was still grilling cheese
and baking hot cross buns
washing our bed sheets
in lavender water

at the end of our first year
the hag had whittled him into a branch
when once he was the tallest tree

he didn't know yellow hair could signal
damage
and she made him tinder
for fire

girls see what men
will not.

On Accepting the Witch's Invitation to Tea

We sealed our fate, easily swayed by her promise of tomato aspic
and finger sandwiches. She loiters by the Beauty Bush,
      pushing her persistence
into surround sound.

In this fairy tale expression, we find out about medieval gory—
      running from shadows
and warts of old ladies, reluctant witnesses
to their vengeful fraying.

When I give the signal, pinch me so I can awaken, escaping Gretel's fate
of not getting that the witch's power wasn't her magic,
      but the pleasure she took
living in a dark house without music or picture albums.

Therapists will surmise she was afraid of rejection.
Wrong: she fried her husband in goose fat and ate her children oozing
with gooseberry jam.

An Account of Loneliness

I watch you
swallowing the moon
but when I look again
it's a crusty rock
you're pushing past your gullet

this is your pearl—

which brings up the matter of animal, mineral or vegetable:

will you tell me a salamander is a tree?

That zinc can become manganese?
Can cobalt be air?
The periodic table is not your à la carte menu

you retort: be satisfied with your carrot, lithium, and fire.

I'll settle into a hard chair and wait for a fly to come make love
to my knee

there is no urgency to change.

Hiroshima, As Told by the Village Prostitute

I am of fire
your indecent desire
bursting from your head

Athena burning
hotter than Hades, I am
your Hiroshima.

The World Is Flat

Andrew Wyeth's grass is just shy
of hay, then there's the girl
dragging the green out of it
while keeping to the parameters of existence
set by the Big House.
Did he mean for her to be absorbed by that sad
tempera paint (probably labeled *ochre*
or *as-I-lay-drying-in-the-sun*)?

He painted the algorithm for light
to alight from her white skin
and refract into the sky
but cannot explain why the world is flat
and how the Devil's bridge came to root
up behind the tool shed.

She is a butterfly
pinned safely in time, like my mother
drawn into a field of waxy flowers
looking out at me with perfect round eyes
and a heart-shaped mouth
formed by my perfect five-year-old
understanding of line and space.

Divine Purpose

old owl
in blackbird territory
shreds air

and stains the sun
with their blood
until he sees

his power reflected
in eyes much smaller
button and black.

Still Life

I drink with myself and for myself.
I drink to my life and to my death.
my thirst is still not satisfied.
        —Charles Bukowski, "a fine madness"

When the siren song
of the Beguiling One,
the Muse of Booze, begins,
it's time to bang kamikazes
down my hatch
until two becomes twenty
(Muses are good at multiplication)
and I'm wearing my typewriter
like a crown of thorns

I'll be a holy man
on the street corner
a drunk bastard howling
at the moon
until it falls
into my pocket

still life with drunk
is not abstract
or Cubist

just existence.

"Jane Austen, reconsider"

writing me into your landscape of petticoats and pianofortes,
please be advised, my party manners are unfortunate.

I will drink all your wine and double dip. Invite me to tea
if you can forego all your layers of etiquette.

Don't you see I would fare better in something Elmore Leonard?
Knocking knees with unrepentant Ojibwe assassins

chain smoking and dusting off a bottle—an anvil
masquerading as a dame?

Have the boys call me Bossy Betty or Luscious Letty,
and make sure they admire my derriere and damsel hair.

Call me gauche, think me brazen. I won't take it as character
assassination. Thank you for the affirmation.

No Regrets

you
stepped out
to get a bag
of ice
from the 7-Eleven
two days ago
without even
a fisheye goodbye
streaked
across the
linoleum

no regrets
because
we both knew
you were a pain
in the ass

I won't
bother
the public
with "gone missing"
posters
taped to lamp posts
and mailboxes—
who will
remember
your brown eyes
were blue?

I will just
imagine you
in between Trenton
and Timbuktu

and if anyone asks
I'll tell them
you found Limbo.

1977: Kiddieland, the Devil and My Dorothy Hamill Bangs

i.

The Ferris wheel and carousel
used to draw them in
now it's down to the clown
in a dress and the midget
fire-eater
to gather the reluctant
into a crowd,
swindle them
into watching
the grotesque pageantry
that is the state
of our humanity:
pennies tossed
into a cup.

ii.

The city is burning
through
a thousand fires,
West 107th Street
goes black
while I sit
under the table
listening to how
menacing empty
spaces can be.
My father's whispers
turn into hissing—
it's the Devil

talking
through him
slithering
into my ear
my brain
and my only
escape is to
slip into
the hole
inside
my head.

iii.

On TV
zombies are
clutching
new sneakers
and heaving
mattresses
over shoulders
not so interested
in my human flesh.
They look like
they are shopping
except you know
they are stealing
because
they are smiling
and not paying
for any of it.

iv.

In the morning
I look to see
if I am a zombie
and find
my Dorothy Hamill bangs
unharmed
and my face
is not
rotten meat.
My father is
in the kitchen
with his head
in our hot
refrigerator.
He pulls out
the peanut butter
and says
Get the bread.

Opus

A simple maiden in her flower
Is worth a hundred coats-of-arms.
—Alfred, Lord Tennyson

Alien
in the land
of dogs and lies,
I am an ordinary bloom
naked and moody
in your garden
of rocks and thorns,
ignored by industrious bees
and copious butterflies.
Your hands revive
what nature would not allow
each finger a moment
of grace
fueling my greed
for more.

Alien
no longer
in this empire
of sinister,
I am speckled and shiny
like a sparrow's new egg.
Friend, you are Pygmalion
with green thumb and riotous eye.
You know me as a sculptor
knows his sculpture,
as a tree knows her acorn.
I match you eye for eye

flaw for flaw
want for want
and I am complete
with my petals
in place.

Peony

Here comes my brother Horse Face
with Butcher's Son and Carpenter Man
to drag Old Widow Lee from her house
she's in her red cloak with a rice sack over her head.
My brother is a strange pick for this kind of work—a sickly baby
grown into a sickly baby. What did they promise him?
Pork fat fried in peanut oil, thick yam cakes
dipped in new honey? His favorite plum wine?

She was Peony
pink petals bursting with pride
when her husband was alive
but when he choked on a walnut and died
they called her witch. Neighbors claimed
she turned sloppy suitors into rats
and ate songbirds to learn their song
her feet didn't always touch ground

but when the town gathers at the square like hungry ghosts
all they will see is an old lady hanging from a tree.

I will be standing in the widow's thick sweet potato patch
wondering if she would miss one or two . . .

Koreans in Proverbs: You Start Real Close

Even a straw shoe has a mate
헌 짚신도 짝이 있다

A Dallas whore
the one you loved
and weaved into
a lore of requited love
left you a note
on her door
on the April Sunday
you'd come to call
with yellow flowers
picked out from
the drugstore.

Did she write
how sorry she was
for leaving you
behind?
That it was for
your own good?
A likely story
found on the pages
of a dime store
novel.

Scratch where it itches
가려운 곳을 긁어 주다

you start real close
circle each other
and give a twirl
if he's able and has stopped
holding a grudge
from the last time
when your stiletto
met his toe

he yelped!
like you'd meant it
but all you wanted
was to merengue.

THREE

KOREAN GROCERY

Mary Talks to God

There beneath an olive tree
We'd offer up our plea
God's creation innocent
His arms surrounding me
   —Richard Shindell, "The Ballad of Mary Magdalene"

Will it and I will
shed this skin
to show you

I was the one
who followed
your son

on the crucifix trail
I knew him
as a man

taking his flesh
as he took
mine

he put
his light
in to me

making me
corruptible
nevermore

I believed
my love
could save

but soldiers came
and took him
while I was

working
dough
into bread

leaving behind
their dead goat
smell

you let them
nail him
down

drain him
of breath
and blood

did not stop
birds from
pecking out

his eyes
was he not
your brightest star?

Golem

resurrected ratio

of flesh to stone

of earth to air

God's tongue

hatching

bones

and woebegone souls

we reap

the first child

of man

to kill all lambs.

Rodney King, Los Angeles 1992

peel
his skin
blessed oblivion

plunge him
into the blood
of lambs

and masters
into the blood
of slaves
and chickens

open up
pulp

open up
memory of the conception
and the flood

let him eat
cake.

Fat and Dust

What if Hansel had accepted
the Witch's offer to supper?
Satisfying her desire to apply
China cups and crisp linens,
ply him with Beef Wellington and
cherry cordial—what she calls *public relations*.
He could have spread the word:
the Witch was misunderstood
scapegoated for every dry season
and cows gone mad.

NO WAY he'd giggled
(she didn't know boys did that)
and ran off in a shudder
of fat and dust. Her story?
She is the only daughter
of a second son, coddled in childhood
fondled in pubescence
growing up to practice pastry
and chemistry with due diligence
on young lads
of good circumstance.

She accepts her nature—
sets out her basket busting with hot cross buns.
Those boys in short pants head
into her larder, full throttle, bursting.

Korean Grocery

The boy I love is a decade younger
and glistens like tuna.
Thursdays he drives in from West New York
(which is really New Jersey)
to sit in a conference room
where a Columbia grad drills us
on indirect verbs.
All the while, the ghost of Anne Bancroft
breathes hot and heavy in my ear
I am here to study the language of my ancestors
but all I can do is ogle
this fine specimen.

How to stop swooning?

After each class
I find myself
in the frozen fish section
pressing halibut
to my hot flesh.

Koreans in Proverbs: One Daughter Is Worth Ten Sons

One daughter is worth ten sons
딸 하나 열 아들 안 부럽다

Rice

grains
must be washed
twenty times
or the spirits
malingering
will get in
you
and turn you
into a hungry ghost

this is a job for girls
not sloppy boys
running around
like headless cocks

(scratching their balls all the time!)

pity their mothers
strapped to babies
trapped in front
of the eternal cooking pot.

Dowry

A man with eyes smaller
than his stomach
will not make it through
winter

he will crow like a handsome
rooster and do nothing
but bring on the evil eye

I will wash him
out of my life

ten hens
eight persimmon trees
fifty sacks of rice
three sows
ten casks of beer
and sixty ri of soft cloth
cannot be squandered
that way.

Promise

The Moon watches
as we fold our pale bodies
into each other.

"I find my father's magazines"

and open up to
women
spun from cotton
candy
gold hair
in both places
like the girl who wanted to eat and get eaten
in that story of the bears

under water
I look at my nipples
brown
hard and alive
I know these
are my true
eyes.

Day of the Dead

In our kitchen sink
blue crabs
from Grand Street
duel a duel
of the damned
till my mother
decides it's time
to take down
her favorite ceramic jar
(the one with the red rooster)
and build her pyramid
of crabs:
the fat
the skinny
the mean
piled up
to meet
eternity
as she pours in
the soy sauce.